Kate Middleton

ABDO
Publishing Company

Big
Buddy BOOKS
Buddy Bios

by Sarah Tieck

Published by ABDO Publishing Company, 8000 West 78th Street, Edina, Minnesota 55439.

Printed in the United States of America, North Mankato, Minnesota.
062011
092011

 PRINTED ON RECYCLED PAPER

Coordinating Series Editor: Rochelle Baltzer
Contributing Editors: Megan M. Gunderson, BreAnn Rumsch, Marcia Zappa
Graphic Design: Maria Hosley
Cover Photograph: *Getty Images*: WireImage.
Interior Photographs/Illustrations: *AP Photo*: Gero Breloer (p. 23), Bob Daugherty (p. 23), Alastair Grant (pp. 11, 28), Fiona Hanson/PA Wire, File (p. 9), Martin Meissner (p. 5), Press Association via AP Images (pp. 15, 19, 21), Stefan Rousseau/PA Wire:9788340 (Press Association via AP Images) (p. 7), John Stillwell/PA Wire URN:10522455 (Press Association via AP Images) (p. 23), John Stillwell/PA URN:10626041 (Press Association via AP Images) (p. 25), Kirsty Wigglesworth (p. 17); *Getty Images*: Nick Harvey/WireImage (p. 9), Indigo (p. 15), WireImage (p. 27); ©The Middleton Family, 2011 (pp. 11, 13).

Library of Congress Cataloging-in-Publication Data

Tieck, Sarah, 1976-
  Kate Middleton : real-life princess / Sarah Tieck.
    p. cm. -- (Big buddy biographies)
  ISBN 978-1-61783-020-4
  1. William, Prince, grandson of Elizabeth II, Queen of Great Britain, 1982---Relations with women--Juvenile literature. 2. Middleton, Kate, 1982---Relations with men--Juvenile literature. 3. Princesses--Great Britain--Biography--Juvenile literature. I. Title.
  DA591.A45W5584 2011
  941.086092--dc22
  [B]
                              2011017208

Contents

Royal Bride 4

Family Ties 6

Growing Up 8

Meeting a Prince 12

A Royal Wedding 16

A New Life 20

Fashion Forward 22

A Duchess's Life 24

Buzz 29

Snapshot 30

Important Words 31

Web Sites 31

Index 32

Royal Bride

Kate Middleton is part of England's royal family. She is married to Prince William, Duke of Cambridge. He is second in line to be king of England.

Many people think of Kate as a princess. But, she is actually the Duchess of Cambridge. As a duchess, she attends important events and does **charity** work.

After her marriage, Kate was often called Catherine or Catherine, Duchess of Cambridge.

Where in the World?

N W E S

Scotland

NORTH SEA

Northern Ireland

UNITED KINGDOM

ATLANTIC OCEAN

IRELAND

Wales England

Reading Bucklebury

Family Ties

Catherine Elizabeth "Kate" Middleton was born in Reading, England, on January 9, 1982. Kate's parents are Michael and Carole Middleton. Her younger sister is Philippa, or Pippa. Her younger brother is James.

Kate's parents met while working for an airline.

Pippa (*right*) and Kate are close. They both enjoy sports and fa[...]

Growing Up

Kate grew up in an ordinary family. They lived in Bucklebury, England. Michael and Carole opened a mail-order party supply company in 1987. They sold toys for children's parties. Over time, their business grew! They were happy to be able to give their family a good life.

James is a business owner. He sells cake kits.

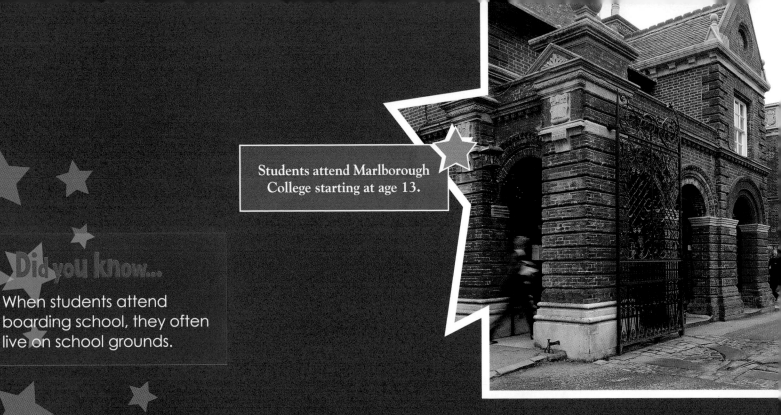

Students attend Marlborough College starting at age 13.

Did you know...

When students attend boarding school, they often live on school grounds.

Kate attended boarding schools as she grew up. She studied at Saint Andrew's School from 1989 to 1995. After that, she attended Downe House School. Next, she attended Marlborough College. All three schools are located in England's countryside.

Kate was a good student. She also enjoyed running and playing sports, such as tennis and field hockey.

Meeting a Prince

In 2001, Kate began attending the University of Saint Andrews in Scotland. She studied art history.

Around this time, she met Prince William. He was also studying art history there. They became close friends. This changed Kate's life. People began to take her picture. And she was in newspapers and magazines.

In 2006, Kate and her parents attended Prince William's graduation from the Royal Military Academy. Queen Elizabeth II was also there.

Did you know...

Queen Elizabeth II is William's grandmother. She became queen of England in 1952. William's father is Charles, Prince of Wales. His mother was Diana, Princess of Wales. She died in a car crash in 1997.

After **graduating** in 2005, Kate worked in fashion. She was a buyer for a clothing company. She also helped out with her family's business. During this time, Kate and Prince William remained close.

Kate and William have much in common. They both like to travel and ski.

A Royal Wedding

In 2010, Kate and Prince William traveled to Africa. There, he asked her to marry him. He gave Kate his mother's **engagement** ring. People around the world looked forward to the couple's wedding!

Kate's ring is a blue sapphire
with diamonds around it.

17

William and Kate's royal wedding took place in London on April 29, 2011. They were married at Westminster Abbey.

The event drew much attention. About 1 million people lined the streets of London to watch. Millions more around the world watched the event on television and the Internet.

After their wedding, Kate and William rode through London in a carriage. William's parents rode in the same carriage after their wedding!

A New Life

After the wedding, Kate's life changed even more. As part of the royal family, she traveled and attended events. She also worked to help people and charities.

People began calling her Duchess Catherine or Her Royal Highness. They bowed or curtsied when they met her.

People gathered outside Buckingham Palace to see Kate and William on their wedding day. Kate appeared to say "Wow!" when she saw how many people there were.

Fashion Forward

Kate enjoys fashion and clothing. Sometimes she wears simple things such as jeans. Other times, she wears fancy dresses and hats. Kate is known for her sense of style. So, reporters often take her picture.

After people saw Kate's wedding dress, many wanted one like it.

William's mother, Princess Diana, (*above*) was also known for her sense of style. Many people say Kate is like her.

Did you know...

Anglesey, Wales, is an island. Wales is part of the United Kingdom. It is next to England.

A Duchess's Life

As the Duchess of Cambridge, Kate's life is different from most people's. She and Prince William attend many events as part of the royal family. They have guards to keep them safe.

Kate and William have a house in Anglesey, Wales. William is serving there as part of the Royal Air Force until 2013.

After their wedding, Kate and William looked forward to their new life together.

Even though the couple lives in the countryside, they often visit London to attend events. They also spend time at the royal family's homes.

When Kate and Prince William have time to themselves, they like to go to Africa and the Caribbean for fun. In summer 2011, they traveled to Canada for an official visit.

After they became engaged, Kate joined Prince William at official events.

When Prince William becomes England's king, Kate will be the sixth Queen Catherine of England!

Buzz

Since her marriage to Prince William, Kate has become very famous. People around the world are interested in her life.

People are excited to see what's next for Kate Middleton. Many believe she has a bright **future** as England's Duchess of Cambridge.

Snapshot

★**Name**: Catherine Elizabeth "Kate" Middleton

★**Birthday**: January 9, 1982

★**Birthplace**: Reading, England

★**Schools**: Saint Andrew's School, Downe House School, Marlborough College, University of Saint Andrews

★**Official Titles**: Duchess of Cambridge, Countess of Strathearn, Baroness Carrickfergus

Important Words

charity a group or a fund that helps people in need.

engagement (ihn-GAYJ-muhnt) an agreement to someday get married.

future (FYOO-chuhr) a time that has not yet occurred.

graduate (GRA-juh-wayt) to complete a level of schooling.

Web Sites

To learn more about Kate Middleton, visit ABDO Publishing Company online. Web sites about Kate Middleton are featured on our Book Links page. These links are routinely monitored and updated to provide the most current information available.

www.abdopublishing.com

Index

Africa **16, 26**

Buckingham Palace **21**

Canada **26**

Caribbean **26**

charity work **4, 20**

Charles, Prince of Wales **14, 18, 19**

Diana, Princess of Wales **14, 16, 18, 19, 23**

education **10, 11, 12, 14, 30**

Elizabeth II, Queen **14**

England **4, 6, 8, 10, 14, 18, 19, 24, 26, 28, 29, 30**

Middleton, Carole **6, 7, 8, 14**

Middleton, James **6, 8, 9**

Middleton, Michael **6, 7, 8, 14**

Middleton, Philippa **6, 8**

Scotland **12**

style **22, 23**

Wales **24**

Westminster Abbey **18**

William, Prince **4, 12, 14, 15, 16, 18, 19, 21, 23, 24, 25, 26, 27, 28, 29**